Words from Stone

POEMS OF WILD PLACES

Martin Salter-Smith

Published by Martin Salter-Smith 2019

First Edition

ISBN: 978-1-9160217-2-3

Printed in the UK by INGRAM

Book & Cover Design by Russell Holden

www.pixeltweakspublications.com

A Catalogue record for this book is available from the British Library.

Also by Martin Salter-Smith:

Gilgarran's Will
Tangled Web
The Spanish Son
Our Stolen Years

Contents

MIRACLE ABBEY

THE WILD PLACES

TIME PASSING

TOWN BOY IN THE COUNTRY

TRAVELS

CHARACTERS

WALKING POEMS

THIS AND THAT

MIRACLE ABBEY

A poetic celebration of the Cistercian presence in Furness

Cold feet

In the year 1127 monks of the Order of Savigny came to the Furness Peninsula to establish an abbey. They had been granted land by Stephen of Blois, who later became king of England, and moved to Furness from Tulketh in Lancashire. The site was so inaccessible it was described as being on an island. Twenty years later the Savignacs amalgamated with the Cistercians and the foundation of the Abbey of St Mary of Furness began its long history, although their first church was a simple wooden building.

⌘ ⌘ ⌘ ⌘ ⌘ ⌘

My feet are cold in this wild place,
remotest site beyond the sands
where we have come to make our base
and build our abbey with our hands.

Beckansgill they called this dale,
valley where the Viking trod.
We will not fear, nor will we fail
by labour here to praise our God.

Few travellers will pass this way
and those who do are hardy men;
our Tulketh home seems far away-
we shall not see that place again.

Beyond the world, beyond the tides
we have embraced this lonely trial.
The Vale of Nightshade's sheltering sides
Conceal us on this wooded isle.

Shifting strands and sinking marsh
have cut us off from England's heart.
Our life is simple, strict and harsh;
our Order's rules set us apart.

Stephen sent us, Savignacs,
before anointment as our king.
In fields we bend our white-robed backs
and in the raftered church we sing.

Our barns with summer's harvest filled,
our sheep flocks fattened as they graze,
we start to cut the stone and build,
and raise our Abbey, God to praise.

Building it bigger

Building the Abbey was a huge undertaking without modern transport methods, machinery, cranes or scaffolding. The stone was sourced locally from quarries at Ormsgill, Stainton and the Vale of Nightshade itself. As the Abbey grew it towered over the tiny houses of ordinary people and all other buildings in the area, The building of the Abbey was in itself an act of faith, not least because some of the architecture was experimental and not always successful.

⌘ ⌘ ⌘ ⌘ ⌘ ⌘

Romans cut quarries, rolled out roads
of steadied stone, for marching men to glory;
built baths and heated houses, fine abodes;
but seldom seemed to aim above one storey.

Norsemen knew wood and shaped it, ships
springing to sea safely on the swell;
houses like hulls, keel-roofed, carved strips
of planks placed as a haven; a home in which to
dwell.

Peasants lived lowly, in hovel or hut,
trimmed turf for roofing on wattled walls;
fear of the forest at dead of dark but
pious praying at noon when the Angelus calls.

Church chimes ring round from frowning towers –
far Furness finds us building bigger.
Sandstone shaped through days and hours;
masons' mallets forming figures.

Riven rock from Ormsgill becomes the biggest building
statues stand in alcoves, altars hushed in awe;
murmuring monks in shadow shrunken down to children;
arches of such altitude were never seen before.

Norman nave nudged into Gothic transition,
pillars point proudly, pushed up to the sky;
labourers climb ladders to lofty position;
on scanty wood scaffolds they must death-defy.

Builders consider and check calculations,
buttresses shoulder the bulge of the stone;
roof-raising blessed with relieved celebrations;
cloister constructed for praying alone.

Nothing so massive had ever been dreamed:
a symphony: stone surging up from the sod;
ambitious devotion dictates our attempt:
Christian monks climbing up to our God.

Miracle abbey

The immense Abbey church, enshrining the latest developments in ecclesiastical architecture, was an enduring symbol of faith and a source of inspiration. It provided a miraculous backcloth to the life of prayer and work adopted by the Cistercians, where monks and lay brothers went about their quiet business side by side.

⌘ ⌘ ⌘ ⌘ ⌘ ⌘

Leaping stones and golden light
Vaulting fanning, soaring height

Norman arch to Gothic point
Dresser's shaping, mason's joint

Carving-crusted gargoyled glory
Every statue tells a story

Plangent plainchant, cloistered quiet
Rough robes, sandals, simple diet

Contemplation on the lawns
Winter midnights, summer dawns

Simple prayer and love for others
Monks at Mass and working Brothers

Tenants live in huddled dwellings,
Clearings cut by ancient fellings.

The Abbey's size sets it alone:
Towering bulk of massive stone.

Stained-paned flood of fractured light
Homage to God's holy might.

Necks crane up to see the roof
A miracle! And this the proof.

Plunderers

Despite its remote site Furness Abbey was not immune to the depredations of thieves and pirates. The Scots, including Robert the Bruce, raided frequently, sometimes coming down the coast to cross the River Duddon. A former monk, Wimund, also caused the Abbey many problems with his raids. As a result of these attacks the castle on Piel Island was built as a safeguard for the monks.

⌘ ⌘ ⌘ ⌘ ⌘ ⌘

Surging through the pebbled Duddon
jingling harness, hoofs that thunder
cold-eyed raiders, swift and sudden-
do they come here seeking plunder?

Forest lends us fuel and shelter,
flocks our source of growing wealth;
robbers ride in, helter-skelter
others take our sheep by stealth.

On Walney Channel shadows fall;
responding to the reach of oars
a boat slides under sombre walls
to lock its load behind the doors.

Piel, our castle on its island,
hides our vestments and our chalice
sea-girt stronghold, solid, silent,
safeguard from the men of malice.

North-west lands are still debated
Bruce's Scots contest the border
pirate prows are never sated
monks no match against the slaughter.

Thieves may take our goods and chattels,
murderers our people's lives;
with faith and fortitude, not battles,
Our community survives.

Abbey Lands Way

Many pack horse routes still criss-cross the lands of Furness Abbey. A lot of these routes were also used by drovers and travellers of all sorts. One route can be traced for about forty miles, all the way from Furness Abbey to Grange-in-Borrowdale, the most northerly farmstead belonging to the Abbey. It passed through Seathwaite in the Duddon where field enclosures had gradually begun to spread further up the slopes, and Brotherilkeld in Eskdale where it crossed the Roman road from Ambleside (Galava) to Ravenglass (Glannoventa). It was not unknown for pack horse trains to vanish in the wild and unforgiving terrain of the central Lake District.

⌘ ⌘ ⌘ ⌘ ⌘ ⌘

A hoof-shuffling leaving of the Abbey's precinct,
panniers packed on ponies taking to the track.
From Dalton to Grange all our lands are linked;
iron brought to bloomeries, fleeces coming back.

Seathwaite in the dale that the Vikings cleared,
new fields patterning the sloping valley side;
a God-forgotten spot till the Normans appeared,
taming the forest where the wild boar hide.

Brotherilkeld where the old Roman road
crosses on its coiling down to the sea
from the fort where cold-legged legions strode
cursing the place that they needed to be.

A long striding by the pony's shoulder
jogging to the jingle of its blaring bells,
toiling to the Hause where the winds cut colder
in the shape-changing mists of the far-flung fells.

Ice pearls the pools on the mud's cold crust
as we move below mountains and snow-sheathed ridge;
nearly in Borrowdale, now we jog just
down to the Derwent and its double-arched bridge.

Wool wealth

The Cistercians developed a reputation for being able to make the most of uncultivated land by raising sheep. In 1242 they added 14,000 acres of Eskdale to their possessions, acquiring the farm now known as Brotherilkeld. This wild and rocky stretch of untilled land might have seemed a strange purchase as it involved the release in exchange of fertile land on the coastal plain around Seton Priory. However, it also provided a crucial link between the Abbey's possessions in Low Furness and its farms in Borrowdale. At the height of its power, Furness was second only to Fountains Abbey, owning 55,000 acres of land. As they grew wealthier, the Cistercians, like the Benedictines before them, began to lose the simplicity of their lifestyle and beliefs. Their growing power eventually made them a threat to the king.

⌘ ⌘ ⌘ ⌘ ⌘ ⌘

We are the tamers of wilderness acres
where clubmoss and lousewort lie close in the grass;
mountainsides, rocky and largely forsaken
where nibbling sheep hear the whispered wind pass.

We gave up our land on the Cumberland coast :
sweet pastures and fields sweeping down to the shore;
for cotton-grass bogs and thick mist like a ghost
and the towering crags where the waterfalls pour.

What can these rock-muscled bracken slopes nourish?
What can survive here when nothing else will?
Cloud-fleeced and stubborn, our Herdwicks can flourish
when nurtured by shepherds at home on the hill.

We are the White Monks, the wasteland improvers,
shearing and harvesting wool by the ton;
flock-bleating sheep-walks and shepherds and drovers
increasing our wealth so tenaciously won.

We are the toilers of meadow and garden,
bending our backs till the long day is done;
but pride in our profits is making us harden,
disfiguring dreams once in beauty begun

Our abbots rule over both village and mountains
corrupting beliefs that we gathered to share.
From simple beginnings we now rival Fountains;
the power of our preaching makes great men beware.

One man's curse

Henry VIII's attempts to bring the church's wealth under state control led to the Dissolution of the Monasteries. The smaller ones went first in 1536 and a year later Furness was the first of the major monasteries to succumb to the radical changes overseen by Thomas Cromwell, Henry's chief minister. Lead was being stripped and windows broken before the last monks had left, and the great architectural achievement of the Cistercians began its long decline.

⌘ ⌘ ⌘ ⌘ ⌘ ⌘

it appeared henry's wife was not what he required
desperate for the sons he never sired
the resolution of his trouble
reduced many a monastery to rubble,
how can the wishes of just one man
result in a religious ban
flesh and blood like the rest of us
not necessarily the best of us
destroyed the abbeys painstakingly built
taxed the abbots to the hilt
changed the history of us all
caused the monastic orders to fall
heritage lost through ambition and power
destoyed in a capricious hour
cromwell the instrument of dissolution
helped the anglican revolution
he made his name while the rest of us lost
our spiritual homes – at such a cost!

abbeys so lovingly put together
with sweat and blood to last forever
destroyed in a moment, destroyed forever
thousands of men to be ruined forever
england's heritage, stone dashed from stone
random ruins left standing alone
masons and carpenters, man and boy
thousands to build, one man to destroy
ecclesiastical elegance:
saved us from growing arrogance
the dissolution could have been worse
suffered under henry's curse
the destruction was merely physical
later, it could have been spiritual
the walls were tumbled, they fouled the well
they quashed the abbey and muffled the bell
acquired the possessions they wanted to sell
forced us from vale of nightshade's dell
we had no home in which to dwell
what is our future? we cannot tell
we left and solemn silence fell ...

Recycling

After the Dissolution of the Monasteries much dressed stone was carted away from the decaying Abbey for building purposes. Many a local farmhouse boasts lintels and other stonework which started life under a Cistercian mason's chisel.

⌘ ⌘ ⌘ ⌘ ⌘ ⌘

Under the changing Northern sky
on Furness fells the farmsteads lie

as if they grew straight from the soil
mute evidence of settlers' toil

but those who built here saved their trouble
instead, purloined Cistercian rubble.

They spared the quarryman his trade
and stole the blocks the monks had made.

St Mary's massive church dissolved
and sourcing building stone was solved:

arches, pillars, pulled asunder –
destroyed, the White Monks' work of wonder.

The peasants took the blessed stones
to build their barns and byres and homes,

the glowing sandstone took their liking:
an early statement of recycling.

They claimed a local privilege
though others called it sacrilege

and every crouched, organic village
was built on monastery's pillage.

The pilfering of stone was shabby
treatment for once-soaring abbey

that roofless under rain and snow
has seen its glass and gargoyles go.

Wraiths of abbots mourn their doom
and haunt the thieving farmer's room

but locked in stonework beauty lies
under the changing Northern skies.

Poet's nightmare

Wordsworth was horrified at the thought of a railway passing through the Abbey precinct. Then again, he considered that painting Lake District farmhouses white was a barbarous, new-fangled fashion. Nowadays a steam train passing through the Abbey grounds would be considered just another part of our heritage. Times change ...

⌘ ⌘ ⌘ ⌘ ⌘ ⌘

He heard the wailing whistle and the squealing of the wheels
gasping through the woodland past the sightless stone,
the sleeping silent shadows now where no monk kneels
and the glassless gothic windows where the breezes moan.

Three centuries of slumber till the abbey had a station;
its majesty had mouldered, just a mossy ruined hulk
but Wordsworth saw it coming and he called it desecration:
engines chasing ghosts away and making poets sulk.

He hates the rails they put in place for iron ore and slate
from Kirkby down to Rampside where the merchant ships arrived;
the coming of the railway line inspired a great debate
but business minds ignored it as the industry thrived.

Today men feel nostalgia when the locomotives pass,
steaming through the hollow where the holy men stood;
a tourist sight now framed within the coach's murky glass:
imagined glimpse: Cistercian cowled by rough white woollen hood.

Wordsworth wouldn't wear it and he called it an intrusion
like the white-walled buildings, just an irritating fad;
nothing lasts forever, and tradition's an illusion;
what we love keeps changing; who can say what's good or bad?

Heritage

The site of Furness Abbey is still a haven of peace and quiet not far from the bustle of the modern town of Barrow-in-Furness. It is difficult now, however, to imagine just how remote this roadless place was when the monks first arrived in the twelfth century.

⌘ ⌘ ⌘ ⌘ ⌘ ⌘

The amphitheatre turns its back
on the spreading sprawl of the modern town
a busy road and a railway track
hedge in the precinct's ancient ground.

Barrow is less than two centuries old;
the abbey dates back to the Middle Ages;
a paradox, if the truth be told:
eight hundred years between these stages.

For half a millenium Furness slumbered,
the abbots departed and silence fell;
then Barrow awoke as the nation hungered
for iron clad ships that they built so well.

The swarm on the bridge at the shift-end hoot
the waving of flags on a launching day
the pride when *Invincible* and *Astute*
slipped into the channel and sailed away

Apprentices learning their fathers' skills
then cycling home through the terraced streets;
a view to the north to the misty hills
from the docks where the heart of Barrow beats.

The clang of the hammers is stilled again,
the ships are few and the town moves on;
but the peace of the Abbey draws women and men
though the church is a shell, and the monks have gone.

Youngsters sledge on the winter slopes,
daffodils bloom round the walls each year,
lovers stroll and discuss their hopes
for the future, while sensing the past is near.

The spirit of calm stalks the ruined site;
in the wind we can hear the ghosts of monks sing;
the trees whisper stories of Furness's might
as we wonder what chapters the future will bring.

Stone Monk

Many a tired walker has had this ghostly experience while coming down by the River Esk as the shadows fall on a late summer's evening ...

⌘ ⌘ ⌘ ⌘ ⌘ ⌘

Descending at dusk below Throstlegarth's span,
treading the turf by the stone-rolling river,
shape-changing twilight; a black hooded man;
frost in the blood and a curdling shiver.

Faceless and ghostly, a monk's eerie cowl
as the good light becomes the last glimmer of day;
dark things of night-time beginning to prowl;
starting at shadows I hasten away.

By moonlight he looms over water and boulders,
a thousand year watch over meadow and stream,
wearing the cloak of the dark on his shoulders;
imagined to be what we want him to seem.

In sunlight he sheds his efficient disguise,
diminished and naked and sadly alone,
and passers-by see with a lurch of surprise
a shattered and lichened and weathered old stone.

THE WILD PLACES

Inspired by the Mountains
...and the Wild Places

Eskdale Ancestors

Folded in the fading purple light I pick my way
carefully down the curving track to end the day.

Sweet scents of bracken blossom on the air
below the buttressed crags where climbers dare.

The darkened dale is lit with scattered lights,
above, the hills are bold, the stars are bright.

High on Hard Knott, Hadrian's stronghold bulks,
where long-gone ghosts and sentries' shadows skulk.

And in the darkened oak wood, leafy drifts
soften my strides amid the moonlight's shifts

The creak of leather, clink of hoof on stone
echo from eras past, though I'm alone.

Murmurs of monks and miners fill my ear;
these medieval phantoms hold no fear.

With vanished troops of folk I tread this track
and sense their spirits smiling at my back.

I cross their bridge, I pass their church,
I reach their ancient inn.
Though generations come between,
these folk were once our kin.

Cistercians

They were always subtle
in their choice of quiet places
unlike the Benedictines,
with their luxurious airs and graces.

Great abbeys grew greedy,
slowly lost their reason for being;
Cistercians tried to find, and show,
a purer way of seeing.

Stephen Harding described
the meaning of true charity;
in those hard times,
such love for others was a rarity.

They started out with monasteries
hidden in quiet dells
but came to own
both Upper Eskdale and the Furness fells.

Their flocks provided wool
that clothed both peasant and knight;
pack ponies carried tons of fleeces
when the trade was at its height.

Whiskered now with reeds,
the ancient sheep-walk walls
moss clad, can still be seen
below the Cam Crag falls.

The closing of the abbeys
prevented a worse dissolution;
to the loss of modest innocence,
is there truly no solution?

Drovers

The sun is sliding down the pallid sky
and subtle snowflakes swirl in sudden squalls.
With aching feet we hasten as we try
to find some shelter by the drove road's walls.

With skins and worn out sacks slung round our shoulders
we drive our cattle to the cold day's end.
The breeze sweeps through the bog and broadcast boulders
until our track begins its downward trend.

Smelling like beasts, unshaven, damp and tired,
we stride between the cattle's swaying flanks.
the hunger of the lowing cows is fired
by scents of pasture from the river's banks.

And as we tend the cattle on their stance
and lengthening shadows cool the twilight air
our calling seems to offer scant romance
with times of rest and comfort short and rare.

But one amongst us finds the life less harsh
and smiling, turns and asks us: "Did you hear
the carefree curlews calling on the marsh
and see the shelduck settling on the mere?"

and as we crossed from Eskdale did you spot
the pink gleams of the granite in the light?
And aren't we lucky now that we have got
the chance to see the moonglow on the height?"

Rough men, unconscious of the mountains' charm,
we pause upon the threshold of the inn,
gazing on him, and one another, with alarm;
then lift the latch, to seek the warmth within.

Pack pony

Day darkens;
the sun, though, still aloft.
Hard going on the track now mired and soft.
Shod hooves and flying sods from yielding ground,
ponies' snuffles,
shouts,
a moving sound.
Anxious to reach the inn,
day nearly done.
Bells jingling,
jaggers at a stumbling run.
Ears pricked, heads bobbing;
straining speed.
Panniers swaying,
goods that people need.
Humped stones that span the brawling of the beck
A pause;
flanks steam.
A pat upon the neck.

(Jagger – dialect word for a packhorseman)

Barn

Outside my window, warding off the wind,
which on a winter midnight madly moans,
the waller's skill, in certainty has pinned
the lichened layers of the settled stones.

A symbol of the world that we are losing,
the wall is intricate but not confusing.

Beyond the silver waters' spreading mouth,
the bulky Combe heaves black against the sky,
and round its foot strange men came, streaming south,
to carve their clearings where the buzzards cry.

By Norsemen, raiding Scots and storms affected,
from round the Combe no good can be expected.

From mist-edged mountain, home of hawk and raven,
peregrine's view of valley and the ridge's swelling;
shelter for sheep and summer harvest's haven,
the fell-braced barn is now a human dwelling.

"You cannot live off views" – the envious voice;
with heart and soul, not head, I made this choice.

Mountain Men

Not for us the stream-side meadows,
cows knee-deep under drowsing elms,
the Norman church with its cool stone shadows,
guarding the ancient village realms;

The cob-walled cottages' pastel shades,
the inn-sign creaking above the green,
the quiet wood and the bluebell glades
where the rooting badger is sometimes seen.

Ours is the higher land close to the sky,
soil drawn thin on its stony breast;
the weary sheep and the buzzard's cry
on the sunset hills of the far north-west.

No fat lands for the ploughman's blade -
the farmer scratching the bones of the earth
the hour-old lamb, still damp, legs splayed,
fearing the fox that watched its birth.

The shepherds' strides in the morning frost;
the vertical crag where the heather clings;
the zigzag tracks where the pack trains crossed
the heights where the quarryman's hammer rings

These are the ridges the Vikings reached
and cut their thwaites in the wooded dales,
turning to look where their boats were beached,
eyes half closed against the gales.

Crib Goch

Tiny, like ants, we crawled upon your flanks
to test our puny courage on your heights,
climbing the sweep of grass to where the cliffs
sprang upward in a sombre wall of stone.
Somewhere a grouse rose, whirring down the slope,
clipping the heather with its trembling feet;
the sound of running water echoed loud
against the silence beating in our ears.
As the gloom of morning blew away
the shattered clouds moved swiftly overhead,
and while the pebbles clinked beneath our boots
fantastic shadows fled amongst the rocks.
Now, as we gained the ridge, with aching limbs,
The wind was clean and cold and bright with sun;
And far below, the lake shone like a shield,
Filling the sheltered cwm with blinding light.
But here we stood, in balance with the earth,
Kissing the very sky with panting breath;
Each side the dizzy cliffs fell steep away,
And we were drunk with air, and joy, and fear.

Rock Face

The rock is silent; the rock does not change;
it is indifferent in its immobility.
Weather can often make it strange
and emphasise our inability.

Secret mists have frequently curled
like demons' breath shrouding the face,
confusing, in this shadowed world,
impressions of height and space.

Water has gleamed on slabs and walls,
numb fingers gripped a tiny hold,
increasing fear of sudden falls:
rain makes us less bold.

Warm rock, and the route is plain;
what of yesterday's fear?
A sudden steepening is serious again:
we are tolerated here.

Evening Hills

The phantom pendant of the bone-white moon
reviews the runnels and the washed-out chutes,
the hillsides scar-seamed like a giant's wounds,
crepuscular landscape bare of brawling boots.

No crowds polluting sempiternal stones,
no fingers pointing south to Blackpool's tower;
as day decays we find ourselves alone
to feel again the silence and the power.

The feet have fled that score the trampled turf,
reaching the valley in the fading light.
Serenity invades the highland earth
and summer's evening slowly sinks to night.

Unpaintable hues in the streaks of the sky,
the sun hissing red in the haze of the sea,
the breeze bends the deergrass and then, by and by,
the mountains are left to the moon and to me.

Wave at Pirnmill

Where does it come from,
hauling from the south
bright breakers foaming at its mouth?
Boat-bobbing, keel-quaking,
driving men ashore,
pushing all before it with its bore.

Curling at its crest
but crawling smoothly through the swell
where it ends no tongue will ever tell:
one wave fetching
all along Kilbrannan Sound
or just a wrinkle where the water frowned?

Abandoned by the dying wind
and left to pass away,
The surface settling to a gentle sway;
one wave subsumed
into the smiling of the bay,
Its power lurking for another day…

Being Welsh

High on Hebog,
hidden in a steep rock tower,
the cave keeps the silent secret
of Owain Glyndwr.
Across Cwm Pennant
weary soldiers seek him in vain;
shepherds shrug mockingly
at the mention of his name.

The old legends
are part of what living here entails;
they hug their history and treasure it,
the brotherhood of Wales.
Their ancient tongue made verses
while the English were still dumb;
despite defeat by Edward,
they never would succumb.

Nursing their wounds,
the ancient kings of Britain
were banished to the hills;
their language was forbidden.
Suspicious of outsiders,
especially their Norman neighbours,
sheep farms and coal mines
became their traditional labours.

Chapel gave them
a stern but guiding creed,
a careful race,
ever circumspect in thought and deed;
a people respectful
of the value of learning.
Hiraeth expressed
the exile's bitter yearning –

not for women in strange hats,
and harps, and bara brith,
but for the essence of the land,
and comrades to share it with.
The surging choir,
sound breaking with a pleasurable shock;
Ffestiniog's stones echoing
to the *drafel* riving rock;

the hawks that circle in the mist
around Yr Wyddfa's peak,
the dragons of Dinas Emrys,
of which the poets speak;
the lonely, ruined hafod,
reed-whiskered in its cwm,
the empty, haunted hills,
heathered and boulder-strewn.

Centuries saw their enslavement;
Saxons and Normans swept
everything before them
till the skies and the rivers wept.
But Welsh hearts hoped again
as the spark of nationhood leaped
and the stones of Sycharth smiled,
where the ghost of Glyndwr had slept.

Windcatcher

the wind is under the buzzard's wings,
and golden gorse is the scent it brings;
the chime in the doorway gently rings,
and it touches the faces of peasants and kings.

it streams out the icy cirrus cloud
and leaves the deer-grass gently bowed,
in the granite gullies it roars aloud,
and billows the sails that the mariners crowd.

But catching the wind? We know it's there,
when we feel it tangling in our hair
but hold it still and you'll be aware
that the spirit has gone, and left ... just air.

Our Place, Our Time

Nothing but ghosts and deep-buried bones
where the grass grows thick round the reed-whiskered stones.
We guess at whose muscle-power made the pit dwelling;
bronze age builders upon the slope's swelling

Monks mined here once, in order to take
the copper they carted to sail down the lake,
loading and floating their boats from the Quay,
unaware of the scale of the diggings to be.

Ground gapes great wounds by the lake-lapping shore,
old workings and winding gear turning no more;
old adits beckon, beams hidden but rotten:
memorials mute now, their function forgotten.

Traders trod trails in an endless course,
crossing bridges that bounded the beck and the force,
and deep in the wood where leaves drift round our strides
the echo of packponies' hoofs still abides.

Pitsteads still litter the quiet forest floor
where colliers burned charcoal to smelt iron ore,
but the hills that once sounded with men in employment
for us are a refuge for peace and enjoyment.

Ruskin the writer removed himself here
in the silence to work on his social idea,
aware of the passions such beauty arouses
at Brantwood, his home and best sited of houses.

James Marshall improved on the landscape he found,
creating Tarn Hows and a view to astound
his guests, after strolling uphill through the stands
of trees brought back from mysterious lands

Arthur Ransome encouraged the children to make
their adventures on hills or at sail on the lake;
his Swallows and Amazons give inspiration
to youthful explorers of each generation.

For this is our playground, our spirit's retreat
where our hearts and our bodies and minds seem to meet;
in this moment the mountains are ours to behold
but we feel a connection with shadows of old

Murmurs of miners and monks fill our ears;
these spectres of long ago holding no fears.
for we are the phantoms the future will know
when like ages before us we too must let go.

TIME PASSING

Reflections on the past and the disappearing present

A Settlement

A bare headland ringed with a crown of trees;
men delved here, raised a homestead on the summit.
Stone walls for shelter, unknown to any ease;
years of wind and weeds have gradually undone it.

Scrub tangled the valleys where the swampland lay;
they chose the high ground for their scanty dwelling –
bronze age weather was better, so they say –
but nights were chill upon the ridge's swelling.

Was feasting held here in a vanished hall?
Were voices raised in poetry and laughter?
History records almost nothing here at all
of how they lived and died and what came after.

Where birch and ash have pushed away the stones,
was this their gateway? This, their outer wall?
And who, amid the ghosts and buried bones
last turned his back and heard the silence fall?

Bridleways

Red dashes on the map betray the line
of trackways threading through the lonely hills.
We need to understand each coded sign
and call upon the navigator's skills

Where droves of cattle trampled down the dale
and ponies' pathways crossed the distant ridge
so little now is left to tell the tale
except some zigzags, and the hump-backed bridge.

Those bridleways today are cut in parts;
the routes that joined the Pack Horse to the Fleece
are swamped by tarmac through the hamlets' hearts
and hard to reassemble, piece by piece.

And yet with care we still perceive the trails,
some sections superseded by the roads;
and where the highway peters out and fails,
go ghostly packmen with their ancient loads.

A trail once led from Ravenglass inland
through Dunnerdale, and on to Thurston's lake
and horses loaded on the western sand
knew well the winding route they had to take.

The grassy road led over Whitfell's side
past ancient homesteads huddled on the moor,
and passing Duddon, weary packmen tried
to bring the goods and news to every door.

From Broughton Moor no bridleway exists;
no hooves will tread again the yielding grass;
the metalled road through Torver joins the lists
of tracks where only shades of ponies pass.

Pause by the bridge and gaze upon this track
and muse upon its layered history,
beginnings hidden as the years stretch back -
once royal route, wrapped in a mystery.

Bridge in a wood

Down from the hills, the hollow-way in the wood
led them to cross the water where they could.
The ford was further down, where drovers waded
and cattle pushed in panic through the flood.

Stones spring now across the narrow force,
above the spume-flecked torrent in its course:
safety for the vital goods they traded
heart-soothing passageway for man and horse.

Romans knew the arch, but left no trace,
no bridge still leaping with unbidden grace
fixed by forgotten hands that laid it
crag-solid but as intricate as lace.

Keystones and parapets in rare conjunction,
its beauty stemming from its simple function
hidden in quiet trees, and subtly shaded;
tribute to medieval men who made it.

Sunkenkirk

Whose fingers touched these stones and felt their weight,
and set them upright in this holy green?
Sunrise gilds them, changing as we wait,
but gives no clue to what this place may mean.

Five thousand years had seen this magic ring
before the Druids brought their bold belief
and touched their harps and taught the Celts to sing
crowned with mistletoe from the oaks in leaf.

As vestments, robes of simple white suffice;
we see their feet tread bare upon the lawn;
sharpening knives for blessed sacrifice;
waiting for sunshafts of the silent dawn.

Which pagans hoped the standing circle would
explain the mysteries of life, and opaque death?
What spirits dwell within this patient wood
or give the wind its sempiternal breath?

We do not know; but we, too, feel the power
held on the cusp between the light and dark.
The world is breathless at this sacred hour
watching the creeping of the shadow's mark.

The warmth of sunlight floods the atmosphere
as night time ghosts let solid shapes intrude;
perhaps the secret of the boulders here
could calm the fears of human solitude.

Light

Luminescence of late light on Western lochs,
Deeply dark stone shadows of the brooding brochs,

Tactile texture of the velvet twilight shaking
On rippled waves like beaten silver in the making.

Filtered, splintered, dappled, swaying beams,
Green light drenching silver birch boles' gleams,

Clouds careering, crossing azure sky,
Ghost shapes grazing hillsides as they fly,

Dying bracken bronzed by golden fire
Emerald moss that hides the quaking mire,

Frosted flagstones sheened by moonlight glow,
While bitter stars across the night sky go.

Light inspires our world, and makes it fuller.
Illuminating rainbow shades of colour,

But take the light! And watch the colour seep
Away to greyness where the shadows creep.

Paddling

All is still; only the dip
of paddles through the burnished glass;
splashed silence as we surface-slip
and watch the lichened islands pass.

Two worlds; below, the waving weed,
the teeming life that needs no air,
the fish on which the otters feed,
the rocks that form the lobsters' lair.

Above, the sun slips down the Sound;
reflections sear our puckered eyes.
Tranquillity and joy we've found
on water under Western skies.

Suddenly by heads surrounded -
whiskered friends with solemn faces;
not by air and sunlight bounded,
predators in deeper places.

Bright-eyed, as if they want to talk,
curious, they close us in.
Clumsy when they try to walk;
gracious when they dive and swim.

Reluctantly we head for shore
gliding on the lazy swell;
paddles pierce the glassy floor
to where the weird sea creatures dwell.

We leave sea-mysteries unsolved,
climbing up the shingled strand.
These are the limits we've evolved –
to stand, feet firm, on solid land.

On the Cliff

Fear-shortened breath upon the footless steep,
no ledge below, illusion of retreat;
clinging improbably on this holdless sweep
of rock; and greater problems yet to meet.

Diminished trees, like bonsai, far below;
the first pitch hidden by the jutting lip;
above the overhang I seek the flow
of upward movement that accepts no slip.

A metal runner eased into a crack,
the rope pulled up and clipped into the wire -
Relief! And now no thought of turning back,
fingers feeling, rock boots stepping higher.

The patient second, hidden on his stance
sees the red rope snaking out of sight;
above, blue sky, grey rock; and soon the chance
to join his leader on the dizzy height.

Balanced between the stone and empty air,
we feel ourselves drawn back by danger's lure;
treading the edge of fear, as in a dare,
what are we doing here, so insecure?

The Barn Owl

Pause as the honking geese beat overhead
shading your eyes to catch the mystic sight;
seek not the secret shores where they were bred,
spending their summers in the northern light.

Touch carefully the rowan's slender bole,
smoothing your hand along its silver bark;
but take no axe to cleave its ancient whole
lest you rouse spirits from the timeless dark.

Deep in the earth, the root, the sap, the seed
have knowledge of the truths that men forgot;
the moving air, the clouds we cannot read
inscrutably ignore our helpless lot.

Strive if you will for secrets that are lost;
search for the meanings hidden from our view;
but shallow human progress has its cost
and nature's ancient links are shown to few.

One Christmas, in the flat December light
walking in fields, morose and inward-turned,
she heard the whisper of the barn-owl's flight
and sensed the mystery for which she yearned.

She heard the ghostly murmur of its wings;
wise-eyed, it paced her home from post to tree.
She dreamed of atavistic, half-glimpsed things,
the panic magic of the woods, the sea...

She sensed the wonder hidden in the earth
Trying to grasp it as she always will;
the owl led surely on towards her hearth
as if to claim the castle on the hill.

Beads

The child looks into the box of beads,
a pile of colours, a vast amount,
and threads them onto the skein of life,
carelessly; too many to count.

Each bead is an endless, wondrous year,
never ending, enough to waste.
Sleeping, playing, watching TV;
time to spare; no need for haste.

For the youth each bead is a passing month
plenty of time for the things he dreams:
books to read and places to go.
No rush; a lifetime's long, it seems.

In the prime of life, so much to do
each bead is a day, its passage swift;
the box's contents nearly spent;
Too late! It's gone, the time for thrift.

The old man's box is nearly bare
the beads are stretched on a worn out thread
too many projects unfulfilled:
time for regrets before he's dead.

Time Passing

No cars came down the lonely lane
to Hywel Rogers' fieldlocked farm;
only the woodpigeons' refrain
disturbed the sultry summer calm.

On market day I watched him pass,
lurching the bumps as Jewel hauled
the cart along the rutted grass;
and smiling; "Bore da!" he called

I saw him return, as evening faded,
The drams betrayed by tuneless song,
to his dreams, not yet – not yet! – invaded
by an outside world that didn't belong.

He belonged, like the mud on his boots,
To the farm his forebears carved from the hill
No Romans or Normans disturbed their roots;
their blood and their sweat can be sensed there still.

The ancient farmhouse and cobbled yard
where chickens pecked for the scattered corn
had barns that remained from a time more hard
their stones set for centuries before I was born.

At milking his head lay along the flank
As he teased out the gift for the daily churn,
Then drove the cows up the meadow bank,
With thanks for the bread that they helped him to earn.

Stooks stalked the field in the waning sun,
stacked sheaves behind the binder's clatter,

and Hywel reaching for his gun
to pot the rabbits as they scatter.

The hayrick grew, a work of art
As pikels flashed against the sky;
Before the baler played a part,
Old skills would keep the fodder dry.

The hand-milked herd, the horse-drawn plough,
The flashing of a harness brass
Have flickered from our memory now
And faded, like last summer's grass …

His son, of a certain generation
Held the past in no esteem
Had no deep felt admiration
For the way things used to seem.

I called at the farm not long ago;
He showed me the caravans in the field
"Diversification! That's how it will go!"
And the shape of the future was there, revealed.

The low white shippon had been demolished:
"You've got to move with the times" he said.
And I saw that the old ways had been abolished
And I knew that Hywel's past was dead.

Good to know …

Mozart's majesty, Shakespeare's plays –
Scraps remembered from schoolroom days;
Jewelled lochs in the long slow light,
Cradling beauty as day becomes night;
The exuberant lark that sings in the sky,
The moist-eyed roe deer, so terribly shy;

The soaring nave and the vaulted roof –
The impossible done, if you wanted proof;
Churchill's speeches and British grit –
Ordinary people enduring it;
A Donovan album from sixty-eight –
Silent grooves in an endless wait …

A name in your address book's pages,
A friend you haven't seen for ages
If you called them, they'd still care –
It's really nice to know they're there.

People you love, who show that they care –
It's really good to know they are there!

TOWN BOY IN THE COUNTRY

Memories of getting to know the countryside

Town boy in the country

The clockless inching of the ochre sun
draws out the light from dawn to dimming day;
the forest and the meadows have begun
to drench his soul with beauty here today.

He knows no name of leaf or tree or grass,
identifies no beast or wandering bird;
the seething city was his only past
and traffic noises all that he had heard.

Stretched in the cooling shade of coppice eaves
he feels the shreds of sunlight on his face,
his fingers touch the mould of fallen leaves,
he hugs the peace of this so secret place.

The warmth of summer hay and buzzing flowers
his beating heart, the breezes in his ear,
warm sun on eyelids; endless silent hours,
serenity he senses stalking near…

The ephemeral noise of the town is starting to fade,
he has found what he needs; he knows this will never pass;
he will dream forever by hill and stream and glade
though as yet he knows no name of leaf or grass.

Space

Here in the heather and the wandering wind
with clouds cantering across the washed-out blue
a great buzzard rocking on its roaming wings
above; but nothing down below to do,

no way of counting out the ticking hours
the high-arcing sun his approximate clock
he cheats the breeze by lying down, and cowers
behind the boulder called the Cowering Rock.

High in the sky a bubbling curlew calls
and the lark lets fall its spendthrift song
across the moorland, snaked with lichened walls
their length unmeasured, as this day is long.

On the gorse with its blowing scent
bees suck the sweetness of the petalled gold
and where the sheep with narrow hoofsteps went
he brushes through bell heather's purple folds.

Long-striding on this limb-springing day
he steps into distance, knowing no mapping sheet,
taking one direction, then another way;
further than any narrow city street.

Climbing a Tree

The ladder of limbs of the sycamore tree
leading him up from the forest's green lightness
lets him rise through the leaves till the earth sets him free
and his eyesight adjusts to the shaft-shifting brightness.

One foot and one hand at a time draw him upward
till he settles himself in a perch like a pew.
Cathedral-like shadows now shrouding the wood;
can any cathedral present such a view?

With gravity mastered he touches the sky
and accepts the soft stroke of the breeze on his face;
unreality fills him now, seated so high,
wrapped in the spiritual peace of this place.

Ethereal dreams till he turns to descend
and sees that the ground has now vanished from sight
the branches that bore him seem now twigs that bend
one slip will engage him in life-snuffing flight.

Hands now like claws and his breath coming fast
legs trembling and ultimate strain on his arms
he climbs down – how slowly! – until at the last
he treads the firm ground with fear's sweat on his palms.

Light and dark

In town there is no dark at night
where street lamps burn incessantly
but here at night the stars are bright
and stud the sky so pleasantly

The ripened moon, a jewelled ball
now draws the light up in its wake
above the marching mountain wall,
above the lapping of the lake.

Yonder where the silence sleeps
the silhouettes of bushes loom
but here the dancing shadow leaps
behind him in the silvered gloom.

As if in some Venetian masque
pale figures move across the lawn
in hueless steely light they bask:
a simulacrum of the dawn

Nothing hurried, nothing rushed
their shadows moving, ghostly, slowly
murmured conversation hushed
in mooncast beams that awe them wholly

And then a dark and cloudy screen
swoops across that shining face
extinguishing what seemed serene
and dragging darkness in its place

The country night now makes him blind
the faded stars have been obscured
he stumbles, terrified to find
a blackness which must be endured

The white of moonlight, then the dark:
he knows now both the two extremes,
no simple strolling in the park –
he knows how to be eyeless seems.

Mr Edwards' Bus

And up the road the laden vehicle labours
'George Edwards' written on its dusty side
crammed with local farming folk and neighbours:
carless people who enjoy this weekly ride.

The bus proceeds as mile slips after mile,
maroon and cream, with long and nose-like bonnet
whose grille and upright headlamps seem to smile
to match the smiles of all the people on it.

Bags and baskets for their Wrexham shopping
and chatter in the ancient tongue of Wales;
the bus forever setting off and stopping
for passengers descending winding trails.

Outside a cottage is a tiny figure;
the throbbing engine lulls us as we wait;
a voice speaks as we watch her getting bigger
"It's not like Mrs Jenkins to be late!"

Turning their shoulders to the sweeping wind
the bent-backed trees that dot the lonely moors
ignore our passing as we slowly grind
over the hills to where the traffic roars.

Here, shops and markets hum with busy bustle
and cafes where the waiters quietly fuss;
how far from where the leafy hedgerows rustle -
how sweet the afternoon's returning bus!

Haytiming

String strung handle of the metal pot
milkless tea in chipped mugs, scalding hot,

tomato sandwiches that hold no meat -
but hunger telling him he has to eat.

The tractor engine stutters to a stop
with smells of diesel and the haytime crop

his palms are burning and his muscles ache
like all the crew he needs this little break.

The loudness of the silence; buzzard's call;
he lounges in the grass where insects crawl.

Heat haze shimmers in the long day's light;
he hopes that all will be gathered in tonight.

Back then, no clatter of a circling baler –
pikels pitched hay onto the labouring trailer.

The dried grass, building to a scented load,
bounced to the farmyard down the unmade road,

where flowers bloom along the trackside edges
and twig-caught wisps adorn the summer hedges

and in the yard the urgent workers toil
determined that the fodder will not spoil.

Hywel rises with the haystack's height
using his skill to make it watertight.

All is gathered; handshakes in the gloom
and weary wending under the rising moon.

Prickled by stalks and reddened by the sun
he sleeps the sleep of one whose work is done.

Den in the wood

Deep in the hush of the heart of the wood
and sheltered by shadows from everyone's eyes
his thoughts turn to tales of the bold Robin Hood
avoiding the Sheriff of Nottingham's spies.

He's an outlaw evading the taking of taxes
hiding, and hunted by land-owning lords
in coppices cut by the sharpness of axes
that the Normans retain at the point of a sword.

Quietly he passes through pale verdant light -
stained glass mimicked by shifts in the leaves.
Bending his bow stave and stringing it tight,
ready to fight now for what he believes...

Treading the forest floor's soft leafy litter
scouting in silence, eyes sharpened but narrow;
unmoved by the sound of the songbird's sweet twitter
putting his trust in his slim home-made arrow.

But a squirrel's swift chattering startles him suddenly;
a clattering pigeon can fill him with fear;
his foot cracks a twig and he stumbles now clumsily
with the startling sensation that someone is near.

But he knows he's alone and he sets to his work,
cutting the hazel wands shaped to their roles,
awestruck by oaks, where the deep shadows lurk
and millennial mosses muffle the boles.

Pitsteads recall here the old charcoal trade;
by the cliff where the limestone lies white as a bone;
a platform he chose, that a collier once made
and built up the bower that he claimed as his own.

With the Winter Cattle

Only the rattle of a restless chain
and the scrape of an indolent hoof
disturb the gloom where the beasts remain
beneath the beams of that ancient roof.

Shrouded in shadows he sits and dreams
far from the worries of home and school;
moments of blessed removal, it seems,
from the dark-clad masters' bitter rule.

The twice-daily hiss in the milking pail
the rhythms that roll round each peaceful day
the steaming of breath and the flick of a tail
and the animals whiling their winter away.

Outside the warm shippen the cold is stark,
the sword points of starlight stabbing the sky
no sodium streetlights destroying the dark
where the outlines of woods and hillsides lie.

A haven, a time from the world, it appears
where Hywel the farmer will welcome him in
a stillness that steadies the rush of the years
where the quiet of the country contrasts with life's din.

In the timeless calm of this rural sincerity
where the tasks of the day are enough for today.
he is sheltered, at peace from the city's celerity,
wistful that life could continue this way.

In the snow

Frosty-feeling faces as they rise
Whitened wonder world around them lies

Silence spread on hillsides, hollows filled
Sound is stopped, the speaking stream is stilled

Fragile flakes fast falling from the sky
No wind to whisk them wildly as they fly

Within, the warmth; and fussing round the fire
With hopes the heat will rise a little higher

Fears that food will not outlast the day
Sent for shopping, soon they make their way

Setting out to stride down to the shop;
Soft snowfall that they hope will never stop

Steps that sink into the settling snow
their traces trod behind them as they go

Fields seem foreign, contours quite confused
A problem finding paths they often used

Clouds are clearing from the sky, it seems,
In blinding brightness of the slanting beams

Painted prisms, diamonds dance for fun:
Crisp clear crystals crunching in the sun

Successful shopping, bread and milk and eggs
Rucksacks heavy now for little legs

Outside, enjoyment leaves the expedition
Clouds coming; cold with no remission

Returning, raw and bothered by the breeze
A lazy wind that lets them have no ease

Their noses run and then they start to shiver;
The stepping stones are slippery by the river

Frozen feet that fumble on the rocks
Snow that slides in boots and wets their socks

Wellingtons that leave the legs rubbed red
Heatless hands and fingers feeling dead

Tears of cold that trickle down their face
Haste to home from this forbidding place

At last! The welcome windows with their light
The fire burning briskly and so bright

Hot tea and scones to savour as they talk
Forgotten now the fearful homeward walk

Hot aches of toes and fingers as they thaw
They hug the hearth and close the cottage door.

Heifer

Loping home down the lightless lane
he saw the lamplight in the barn
he heard the heifer low in pain
as if she suffered grievous harm.

A tableau framed beneath the roof
men frozen from activity;
they contemplate the bitter proof –
a mock made of nativity

They haul with ropes, and as they try
they see the hooves, they see the head
he turns away and starts to cry
in anguish, for the calf is dead

At home he spurned the evening meal
dwelling on the death he'd seen
in shock that such things should be real
a nightmare driven through his dream

He heard his mother, horrified
"He should not see such things, the lad"
His father, thoughtful, simply sighed:
"He's learning. Life is good – and bad..."

Dreams and myths

"Be back for lunch" his mother calls
as he steps away from the world of home;
but a bowshot from the cottage walls
he enters the land where the legends roam.

Red cross knights and bold seigneurs
with burnished helms in the sunlight's flame,
the sere grass brushing their urgent spurs
across the fields at a canter came.

He saw the blazoned banners fly -
through dreaming eyes, all this he saw -
he heard King Harry's rousing cry,
believed himself at Agincourt.

But drawing back within the wood
and drawing back from Norman times
he glimpsed the place where Merlin stood
with Arthur, wreathed with Celtic rhymes.

Bold Bedivere and Lancelot,
their clashing blades and mythic deeds;
the fated Lady of Shalott,
her dying progress through the reeds.

And Tolkien taught him tales of elves
where magic weaves a wizard's world:
the hobbits fate - to find themselves,
and fell-faced riders, flags unfurled.

Here and there he sought the stories
legends, myths and real folk;
Britons, Vikings, former glories
long before the Norman yoke.

And on the moor he sensed the thunder,
heard the tramp of ghostly feet;
Saxons? He could only wonder;
pople he could never meet.

And as he trod the forest floor
where branches breathed of mystery
the past had locked its silent door,
sunk in the hush of history.

And at the house, his mother waiting;
a scolding calming his elation.
No future now in his relating
the world of his imagination.

TRAVELS

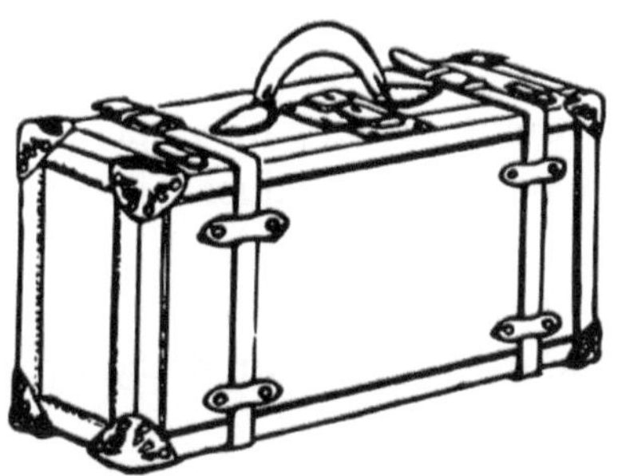

Impressions of different countries

In Spain...

Old Spain?

Weary, coming down from the Pyrenees
from high passes known to smugglers and refugees,

rucksacks heavy now, straps tugging at our shoulders,
seeking rest from the ranges full of ice and boulders,

the moon luminous and the stars like gypsies' eyes
gap-toothed mountains etched like saws against the skies;

soft footfalls in the velvet shadows of the street,
a quiet "hola!" spoken by the villagers we meet

light spilling from within a partly opened door,
rough tables, wine-jugs, sawdust on the floor;

faces lined and brown as the baked earth of the meseta,
glasses of home-made pacharán bought for ten pesetas;

hot beans and spicy sausage served on a massive platter,
contentment found amidst the noise and clatter;

voices, old songs, the thrilling of the strings;
the peace that rest, after exertion, brings;

this was the old, the mysterious, the proud Spain -
and yet, years later, where will we search for it again?

In glass canyons, where the old man in the beret of Navarre
who ran the bulls at San Fermín, now fears the car?

That stern nobility is gone; instead we meet
cranes pecking the bones of old pueblos in the heat.

Meeting Paco

An old man and a mule on an ancient track
"They have gone, "he sighs, "they will not be back."
His arm sweeps down the mountain to the sea
"There is the future of Spain, not here with me.

"Here where our blood mingled with the reddened soil
they were born, but turned their backs on endless toil
under the parching glare of our southern sun
and the blade-thin winds when winter has begun.

"Where the agile ibex scrambles, scattering loose stone
the fincas crumble quietly, and I find myself alone.
No longer mule-back panniers sway and gently push
against the rascavieja and the spiny cistus bush

The ways into our mountains will vanish soon forever;
people will come, and wander, but I know that they will never
see again the packhorse trains heading for Granada.
They turn their backs; they say that life up here is harder"

His features were burnished like his boots of Spanish leather,
darkened but unbeaten by the implacable weather;
Yet behind the bitter smile I thought he would weep soon
under the gipsy stars and the silent moorish moon.

Coming down to San Nicolas - 1980

Over the border at last and the world changes
crossing the snow-pecked Pyrenean ranges
into the heat and a long dropping to the river
looped in green pastures like a serpent's shiver.

The bridge at San Nicolas, stone and sprung arch
signals the end of our frontier-vaulting march.
Spain! Dark land of multi-coloured dreams –
no better way to enter it, tonight, it seems.

The posada dim and cool after the scorching heat,
red wine in an earthen jug, a dish of callos to eat
served by a dwarf; and raucous Spanish speech –
this is the heart of the land we hoped to reach.

The tapestry of old picaresque tales was here:
absurd Quijote seeking his lady Dulcinea,
Lazarillo in the gutter; the adventures that he made;
castanets and quarrels and the moonlight on a blade …

Later we swim in Ara's stream below the bridge
gazing up to the sierra's high serrated ridge.
Africa begins here, they say, under this sky:
we sleep now in Aragon while the night breezes sigh.

Costa

They sleep still in Marbella and in crowded
Torremolinos
no morning sun disturbing their alcoholic slumber;
only the wakeful goatherd in the morning dew has
seen us
leaving behind the Costa and the autovia's
thunder.
Where is the dark silent road, the men on their
donkeys and mules?
The huddled white hilltop village, the women
dressed only in black?
Modesty, honour and pride controlled then by
different rules ...
but that was the land of the past; we can never go
travelling back.

Return to the past of the sixties? Memory will
never now let us
though the multiple threads of the past are never
too distant in Spain.
A bright fire of wood on a beach and eating fresh
sea-caught chanquetes ...
that country is gone, that time too: we shall not see
that country again!

But here, high up here in the campo
the present is like going back
though hoofs seldom spark on the boulders
and bushes crowd in on the track

yet the cabra montés are still startled
and the vulture's wings hover in threat
and the blue of the sky is still silent
and the power of the mountains lives yet.

Montségur

What mercy? Just to pile the fresh-cut wood
that green, produced the acrid billowed smoke.
This way they showed what tenderness they could:
before their victims burned, they let them choke.

The pope of evil proved the truth they told,
(these men of peace who did no-one no harm)
that here on earth the hatred must unfold
because they caused the church of Rome alarm.

The sound of songs beneath the southern sun
the smiles and chivalry and courtly love
the jongleur's tales at night when day was done
the comfort of the castle's keep above;

all swept away by bitter northern knights,
implacable, but this was no crusade;
they may have scorned the South's religious rights,
but seized their lands by fire and bloody blade.

Persecution drove them to the peak
that overlooks the town of Montségur
where warriors came, defenders of the meek
who for a while believed themselves secure.

But in the end their castle was thrown down
and Christian crusaders killed and burned;
two hundred in a meadow by the town
so that their message should be cruelly learned.

What message? Just that Christianity
believes the mantra that "Thou shalt not kill"
unless their priests decide to slay, not pity;
a bitter message here remembered still.

Berbers

Voices echo down the ochre stones
picking through the landscape's tortured bones.
Scorpions shuffle in the shimmered heat,
pebbles shift beneath the sandalled feet.
Muleteers descend the twisting trail
to camp, as copper skies begin to pale.
Bursting green betrays the hidden well
and black felt tents where Berber nomads dwell.
A scrawny goatherd scans his shifting flock
in purple twilight shades of sand and rock.

The crumbling kasbah hugs its history
dust to dust – eternal mystery.
Sheikhs and generals sought to take their land –
remotest range before Sahara's sand.
Below Bou Gafer cartridge cases lie,
mute witness to the death beneath this sky.
To proud old ways the mountain tribesman clings;
once colony, but never bowed by kings.

CHARACTERS

Thoughts on various well-known people; both real and imagined

Wordsworth

Perhaps he wrote too much, too many words
jostling for their moment on the page
fluttering in his head like flocking birds
unwilling to be cornered in a cage.

Slow striding on the hills and bowed in thought;
then, by the fire, pregnant with recollections
his sister scribing images he caught
his inspiration honed by quiet suggestions.

He loved the Lakes, found joy in setting down
the memories of youth he wished to capture
tales of the mountain men and their reknown
rolled round his mind, beloved scenes of rapture

Lines though, not always taut with inspiration
not powerful, like his strides, but slowly plodding
stumbling to include too much information:
over his pages we find that we are nodding;

but when, with passion, loud he thunders:
"Bliss was it in that dawn to be alive!"
awestruck we wait his words, for surely this
is the heavenly voice for which all poets strive.

Ruskin

Slowly as the sunlight sinks to night
and lightshafts splinter in the dimming dusk
he totters to the turret for a sight
of how the somnolescent water looks –

tonight not burning with celestial fire ,
as brimmed his brain with thoughts that knew no
brake;
now his imagination starts to tire
soothed by the timeless lapping of the lake.

Thoughts once pursued him down the dreaming years
thoughts that marked him from his peers as – strange!
A social revolution of ideas
a blood-red tide of visions for a change.

Beauty he sought, and meaning, in each life;
nobility of working wood with hands,
respite from industrialisation's strife,
the right to share the mountain's lovely lands.

But in his home, best sited of all houses
weary now he stands and vaguely peers
where moonlight streaming on the water rouses
a piercing beauty, but now blurred with tears.

At Burgh-by-Sands

So far from home under these Northern skies
where estuary sandbanks meet the plain
the great king, Edward Longshanks, lonely, dies;
his iron fist will not be clenched again.

His castles crushed the warriors of Wales
a monument to conquest in their stones
but here this pillar, lichened in the gales,
reminds us of his worm-infested bones.

Shaping his kingdom, England, to his will
Scotland's hammer, Wallace's nemesis
worthy of crowns and filled with valour, still
a man, and at the last it comes to this.

Forgetting now his kingdom-carving deeds,
we stand by Solway's careless rolling wave
reminded by his obelisk in the reeds:
even the great lie lonely in their grave.

Pottering

Small creatures developed and peopled her page
their characters drawn out by paintbrush and pen
a woman at work in a masculine age
her talent devalued by arrogant men.

Observing, and practising deft brushstrokes;
a self-taught talent and quite unique
her perfect pictures and gentle jokes
made stories to smile at, but tongue in cheek.

Rubbing shoulders with painters – a privileged life;
but constrained by the rules of a stern middle class
sheltered from poverty, hard work and strife
but dismissed as only a day-dreaming lass.

Persevering with painting and finally published
her books were imbued with her love of the Lakes;
their reception was everything she would have wished;
and the freedom a personal fortune awakes!

Unnumbered children are raised on her books
her writing and painting showed off a rare skill;
she captured in colour how the Lake District looks
and ensured by her acts that it evermore will.

A sheep-farmer crammed in a shapeless hat
nurturing Herdwicks and buying up farms,
saving the landscape off her own bat,
halting developers' greedy alarms.

One legacy lying in Peter the Rabbit
another the land that she saved for the nation
where visitors come from affection and habit
to share in the joy and the celebration.

Mary at Framlingham

Around her all the silence lies;
hands clench the parapet's stone.
Peering with dry and straining eyes;
a Queen, or a traitor, alone?

Smoke rising thin from a dwelling,
a peasant out tilling his field;
beyond, is support for her swelling?
Will John Dudley yet force her to yield?

Cast out by her father; betrayed;
usurped by the lady Jane Grey
she waits; what decision is made?
Which way will her countrymen sway?

Her noblemen gather around her
their standards aloft in the breeze …
the herald reins in; he has found her;
in thanksgiving she sinks to her knees.

Elizabeth at Tilbury

Splendid on her saddled steed
rousing the courage of the ranks
a lioness in this hour of need
while Francis Drake earns England's thanks.

On bended knee they hear her words
"...the heart and stomach of a King..."
Against their shields they shake their swords
and loudly let their challenge ring.

But in the Channel English ships
undaunted, drive away the Don;
defiance drums from English lips
and cheers that say the threat is gone.

Elizabethan epic stories;
myths of Merrie England's days
the sceptred isle's imagined glories
gone now – yet the memory stays.

Lanercost

I'm a canon, not a friar;
a job for life; I'll not retire
from praying for the local squire.
St Augustine, I do admire
and I like singing in the choir
beneath the tower (we have no spire).
But life here can be rather dire
and praying often makes me tire;
I hate the scratchy wool attire;
the food is poor – I'm not a liar!
And so to better I aspire
and hope to move myself up higher
to gain the comfort I require,
the warmth I'm waiting to acquire
on winter nights in this northern shire.
The Prior's job is my desire
as he is always warmer, drier
because, as resident high-flier,
only the Prior
is allowed a fire...

The Poacher

The poacher deep in the night-time wood
met the lord of the manor who loudly said
"Get orf my land! You're up to no good.
You deserve such a beating you'll wish you were dead!"

"And what makes you think," the poacher replied
"That you have a right to tell me to leave?
I've wandered these woods since I was a child;
I've as much right as you to these lands, I believe!"

"When the Normans came over with king and with prince
my ancestors fought for this land," said the lord
"And it's been in my family for centuries since,
this land that we won at the point of the sword."

"You say that your ancestors once had to fight for it,
but what did *you* ever actually *do* for it?
And if just being strongest gives you the right to it,
take off your coat, then, and I'll fight *you* for it!"

A Wedding Poem

Endlessly (For Rachel and Chris – 12th September 2009)

High on the mountain and seen by no eye
Clouds are gently releasing their raindrops
Turf makes a waterbed, liquid and earth;
Water, embraced by the land, forms a spring
Where water meets land then a river is formed
The two come together and cannot be halted
The stream makes the valley and gives it direction
The valley supports it and shelters the stream
Quietly weaving a way down the hill
Working together and forming the route
Tumbling and laughing, unsullied and clear.
But lacking the stream there will not be a valley
And lacking the valley the stream will be lost
Sometimes the stream takes a fantasy turn
The valley, confused, tries to bar it with rock
There is turbulence then, and some indecision
But the stream still continues its course anyway,
Headstrong and leaping and sparkling and spreading
In breathtaking waterslides, stream nearly shattered
The anxious long fall to the darkling pool,
Tranquilly sheltered in strong arms of rock.
See I have caught you after all.
Together onwards, pace slowing as the lower lands are reached
More figures by the waterside, fields and towns
Churches and houses by the water margin
Many people entering the scene, children and adults
Some close, some further away
Here is the public place in the world
As the river and valley broaden
But still meandering and curving as they seek the true way
Then strong and purposeful at last to the distant sea
Through the salt marsh of sorrows
And the bright flowers of joy
where water and valley are one.

WALKING POEMS

(or, something to take your mind off it!)

Are we there yet?

Are we there yet? The question that everyone asks:
How much further? the walkers are wanting to know
Are we going up there? Such a difficult task!
If you want to get up there just get up and go!

Are we there yet? Oh no, there are miles still to go;
Will we be there by dark? Not stood here, no we won't;
we must keep on together, not too fast, not too slow -
we shall never get there at all if we don't.

Are we there yet? Oh no, it's around the next bend.
But we can't see what's there or how far we must go!
Just keep on enjoying the journey, my friend
For when you arrive, I assure you, you'll know.

Geological interlude

Here in this remote location
outpost of this island nation
rock gives us an intimation
of the truth of glaciation,
sempiternal operation
moving on without cessation,
ice's muffled crepitation
sliding to its destination.

But imagine our elation
as we walk with trepidation
to see a geological quotation
which, without exaggeration
is worthy of a great ovation.
Not a recent installation
made in shoddy imitation;
no! We gasp in admiration
at a finely formed striation.

Leader's Lament

This group of mountain walkers are a rather funny bunch,
they've hardly set off hiking and they want to stop for lunch
frittering their time away with a sandwich or a bun
in sheltered rocky corners they love basking in the sun.

Returning, they have tales to tell of biting northern gales
snow showers flying from the fells and whipping down the dale
of rocky slopes and icy streams and high and scary ridges
and crawling round on hands and knees beneath the packhorse bridges.

When we go up the voices start a ritual complaining:
"This is too steep we haven't had the necessary training"
and coming down they say the path is "rocky, rough and laming
and mumble that they know exactly "who they will be blaming.
and on their feedback form they say that they will all be claimi
my jokes no longer seem to be sufficiently entertaining

But when the walk is over and they're settled with a drink
and they've had time to rest their legs and have a little think
through half-closed eyes they see again the sunlight on the summit
and know with satisfaction they can say once more "I done it!"

Leaving the mountains

You know you are leaving the mountain
to enter the valley below,
when the women start smelling of perfume,
and nobody says hello.

You know that most folk on this track
won't even get up to the tarn;
they soon will be heading back
for a pint in the Stickle Barn.

Yet you know on a windswept summit
or walking a rocky ridge
that you and the others are sharing
a wonderful privilege.

And you know that the hordes in the valley
will never explore very far;
most will never go further
then two hundred yards from the car.

You know that we shouldn't question
the style and the acts of the tourists,
so why does their clamour unsettle
the old-fashioned mountain purists?

We know if we keep to wild country
we stay easily out of their way
and can still experience solitude
on Bank Holiday Monday in May.

Thousands may come with their families
on a pilgrimage born out of habit;
but how can we blame them for wanting to see
the birthplace of Peter the Rabbit?

Song of the Pyrenees

We've just got back from the High Pyrenees,
and as you will know, in mountains such as these,
it can be terribly hard on the feet and the knees
especially when crossing those difficult screes.
but the hillsides are covered with beautiful trees
and the heat is dispersed by the fresh mountain breeze.
You can swim in the lakes (get in by degrees!)
but in winter I think you will find they all freeze
and you'll need to be wearing your snowshoes or skis.
The mountain hotels have very few fleas
(despite Belloc's warning) to tickle and tease.
The refuges charge only moderate fees
but not all have hot water showers for your ease
and some of the bunks can seem a tight squeeze,
though all have toilets to go to for wees,
and the three course meals have you asking "More,
please!"
Unlike in Nepal, you will catch no disease
and the altitude won't make you struggle and wheeze;
you can see all the things that a traveller sees,
or order some drinks – seven coffees, two teas.
So what could be better, the group all agrees,
than spending some time in the High Pyrenees?

THIS & THAT

The Photograph

The old man said "It's colder today"
as he bought his weekly loaf of bread,
but the shop assistant had turned away
so he pulled his collar up to his head,
walked into the street so bleak and grey
where the dark clouds squeezed upon the town
and the snow began to tremble down
and two days later he was dead.

"Hypothermia", belated officialdom said
when they broke the door of his terrace in
and found him huddled upon the bed
with the ghastly pallor upon his skin.
But he died without hope in this civilised land
And lay there unnoticed for over a week;
The stains of his tears were still on his cheek
And a faded photograph in his hand.

Inner City

This afternoon I saw a sad old man
walk through the smoking rubble of his home
while demolition men stood by and laughed,
then turned away, uneasy at his grief.
Pausing, with eyes half-closed, he seemed aware
of children playing in the cobbled streets,
the scent of spices blowing from the docks,
and women chatting as they scrubbed the step.
Again, he saw himself returning home,
the breezes from the river at his back,
greeting his neighbours as he climbed the hill
to join his family for the evening meal.
Two up, two down, the little terraced house
cradled the only life that he had known;
but as his years ran out, that happy street
was classed as unhygienic, and condemned.

Now he returns, as evening dims the sky,
across the city to some bleak estate,
into his purpose-built old person's flat,
sentenced by mindless councils, to exchange
the friends and the surroundings that he loved
for scrawled graffiti, gangs and broken lifts.
And when he dies, uprooted and alone,
locked in the prison of his tower block,
he hears the city groaning in the night,
choking on the ruin at its heart.

Monday

Silent couples holding hands
in pretentious pubs seem fearful
that the music, like a vague voyeur
will overhear their secret words,
and commune with apologetic beer-glasses
(drinking is a good excuse for not talking
but not for not thinking.)
Older men in quasi-jovial groups
Fondling their tankards like old lovers
Refuse to compromise themselves
But then nobody has much to say on a Monday;
we've just turned over a new week
and nobody's quite
made up their memory.

Remembrance Day 1968

Old men, bowed heads and bugles singing slow
remembering our heroes who have died;
those sons and brothers gone so long ago
to fight for freedom, falling side by side.
Perhaps we wondered why they wished to go;
then somewhere in the crowd a baby cried.

Tommy's Homecoming 1918

These are the years that the Boche has stolen,
years that should have been yours and mine
and the moments and hours that could have been golden
are drowned in the tears of this terrible time.

The grass will grow over the shell-hole and crater;
I won't waste our future in hating the Hun.
Our life as a family is starting much later,
but I know what I'm doing just had to be done.

In the years of our freedom I know I'll be counted
as one of the millions just doing his bit
and I know that I'll wonder to what it amounted –
billets and movements and blancoing kit.

Then I think of the War and the memory lingers
of comrades and strangers all willing to die
for justice, for honour – is this really why?
....Or your breath on my cheek and the touch of your fingers;
my smile at the sound of our son's lusty cry.

Save Our Forests!

(Written when our elected government was proposing to take our forests off us and sell them to capitalist speculators.)

I've been sitting trying to write some verse
but it seems to be going from bad to worse
I want to write one of those Lake District poems
about the hills where the Herdwick roams
and the slanting sunlight that shines on the water
(the things that attracted Mr Potter's daughter)
Wordsworth is in it somewhere I suppose
walking around in his old-fashioned clothes
and Coleridge bravely descending Broad Stand
dare-devil, taking his life in his hand
Ransome introducing the Amazons and Swallows,
the adventuring onto the lake that then follows
the slumbering churches now centuries old
founded by wealthy philanthropists' gold
displaying their blazons of lions and lozenges;
the Turner-like sunsets of reds and of oranges
the changing of colours that evening can make,
Ruskin surveying the length of his lake,
risking the chances of some notoriety
as he formulates thought for a change in society
but most of the beautiful Lakeland lands
are still in a few rich landowners' hands
since the Norman conquest it's been inherited
a fact that makes me most dispirited
Canon Rawnsley, Mrs Heelis were both quite robust
in their work to establish the National Trust
and the Forestry Commission, though making mistakes has
become an essential part of the Lakes
the introduction of access land

strengthened the ordinary walker's hand,
more acres available now to the nation
to indulge in all sorts of outdoor recreation

and now they are wanting to take it away
and sell it to people with power to pay
the Lakes are not theirs to sell or to buy
we stand firm and say: Oh yes? Let them try!

www.ingramcontent.com/pod-product-compliance
Ingram Content Group UK Ltd.
Pitfield, Milton Keynes, MK11 3LW, UK
UKHW040010200726
13854UKWH00001B/133